THE
NATIONAL
GALLERY

GET COLOURING
WITH
Katie

Today Katie is visiting the National Gallery
– and you're invited too! The gallery is
Katie's favourite place to be because, for
her, the paintings really come alive.
All you have to do is pick up your
colouring pencils and follow Katie to
discover the magical world of art.

JAMES MAYHEW

ORCHARD

Self Portrait in a Straw Hat

Elisabeth Louise Vigée Le Brun

"I wonder who this lady is," says Katie. "She must be an artist with her colourful paint palette. That's given me an idea. I know what we can do today . . . let's get colouring!"

Can you colour in her frame too?

A Still Life of Flowers in a Wan-Li Vase
Ambrosius Bosschaert the Elder

"Did you spot the flowers in her hat?" says Katie.
"I'd like to colour a whole bunch of flowers next!
If you look at this painting very closely, you might
see some little insects hiding too."

Be careful
with the delicate
details.

A Wheatfield, with Cypresses
Vincent van Gogh

"Oh look, more flowers," says Katie, "but I think the sky needs a touch of colour! It looks like a storm is coming with all those swirly clouds. I hope it isn't going to rain . . ."

Can you make the sky all swirly?

Mr and Mrs Andrews
Thomas Gainsborough

"Maybe that's why these people are sheltering under a tree. They look very grand with their smart clothes."

Try using dark and light shades for the folds of her dress and add your own background.

How many shades of green can you use?

Surprised!
Henri Rousseau

"It's certainly stormy in this jungle," says Katie, "and there's a tiger stalking through the grass! I have just the right orange for his fierce stripes."

Saint George and the Dragon
Gustave Moreau

"This dragon looks a bit scary too," says Katie. "But brave Saint George is coming to the rescue! Look at the painting – can you see the princess and her castle?"

Draw some scales on the dragon's wings.

The Wilton Diptych

"These angels have such soft, feathery wings compared to the dragon. They just need some colour then they're ready to fly."

Try shading the wings very softly.

Lady Cockburn and her Three Eldest Sons
Sir Joshua Reynolds

A Woman and a Fish-pedlar in a Kitchen
Willem van Mieris

Try using your brightest colours for the parrot's feathers!

A Lady with a Squirrel and a Starling
Hans Holbein the Younger

Cenotaph to the Memory of Sir Joshua Reynolds
John Constable

Men of the Docks
George Bellows

"These horses must be helping the men," says Katie. "I'm going to help too and colour them in!"

Use your blue, green, brown, black and grey pencils to colour in the men's clothes.

Bathers at La Grenouillère
Claude Monet

"That's given me an idea," says Katie. "I think I'd like to colour in some boats. Doesn't this painting look nice and summery?"

What colours would you like the boats to be?

Bathers at Asnières
Georges Seurat

"These people are enjoying the sun too – even the little dog. I would love to go for a swim, just like in the picture . . ."

Try colouring in with lots of little dots – just like the artist!

The Umbrellas
Pierre-Auguste Renoir

"I think it's time to go," says Katie. "You might need your umbrella – it can be very rainy in London! Do come back to the National Gallery soon. You never know what adventures you might find there."